DER

tree top
decorations

tree top decorations

25 dazzling ideas for angels, stars, ribbons and more

EMMA HARDY

CICO BOOKS
LONDON NEW YORK

Published in 2008 by CICO Books
an imprint of Ryland Peters & Small
20–21 Jockey's Fields, London WC1R 4BW

www.cicobooks.co.uk

10 9 8 7 6 5 4 3 2 1

A CIP catalogue record for this book is available from
the British Library.

ISBN-13: 978 1 906094 78 2

Printed in China

Editor: Marion Paull
Designer: Roger Hammond
Photographer: Debbie Patterson
Illustrator: Michael Hill
Templates: Anthony Duke

contents

introduction

Christmas wouldn't be Christmas without a beautifully decorated tree. The tradition dates back to the sixteenth century and originated in Germany, where trees were often decorated with paper flowers, nuts and fruits.

Christmas trees were introduced to England in the 1840s when ornaments made of gingerbreads, and of wax, became popular, and the custom soon spread to America, brought by German settlers living in and around Pennsylvania. Candles were used to add sparkle until, in the 1890s, electric lights provided a much safer and troublefree way to illuminate the tree. The Victorians enjoyed decorating their trees with ornaments that were often home-made, including glass baubles, small toys, beaded garlands and sweets.

The idea of special tree top decorations may have originated with the creation of a gilded tin angel, sometime in the eighteenth century. The story goes that the daughter of a master craftsman died tragically, and appeared to her father in a dream, dressed in gold. So the next day, the craftsman made a tin doll clad in gold, and carved a wooden face to look like his beloved daughter. It being Christmas, his wife placed the angel on the top of their tree. The craftsman's friends encouraged him to make more angels and sell them at Christmas markets, and so started the tradition.

These days we have a wide and very varied selection of tree top decorations available to us, although the traditional angel is still very much a favourite. With this in mind, I have put together 25 projects using many different materials and styles. I hope that the tree top decorations you choose to make will become much-loved family heirlooms, ceremoniously unwrapped each year to take pride of place at the top of your tree, enjoyed and admired by all who see them.

the projects

From glittery angels and beautifully beaded snowflakes, to elegant foil flower bouquets and charming ribbon rosettes, there is a project here to suit every style and theme of tree. Each one is accompanied by illustrated instructions that will lead you step by step through the creative process, and photographs of the finished decoration show you what you are aiming for. A list of the materials used to create each one is provided, although you can make something unique by substituting items on the list for other materials.

None of the projects requires any complicated skills or knowledge and they can all be completed in a relatively short time. The finishing touches will make your decorations truly special, with beautiful buttons, beads and ribbons adding the perfect final flourish.

glittery angel with wire wings

MATERIALS

Fine white net

Scissors, needle and thread

Newspaper

Masking tape

PVA glue, bowl and water

Gouache paints for skin and features, and paintbrush

75cm (30in.) length of dark brown ric rac

Small silver sequins

Thin wired tinsel, about 180cm (70in.)

Wired velvet ribbon

This glittery angel has a painted papier-maché head, but a large bead could be used to make it simpler. Delicate wings are made from fine tinsel to add sparkle – wired tinsel is best, so that the loops hold their shape.

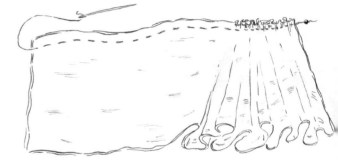

1 Cut two layers of net measuring 110 x 18cm (43 x 7in.). Lay one on top of the other and sew running stitch about 1.5cm (¹⁄₂in.) from the top through both layers. Gently pull the thread to gather the material to make the dress. Finish with a few stitches to prevent the gathers pulling out.

2 Make the head by scrunching up newspaper, and secure with masking tape to hold the shape. Roll up a small piece of newspaper to make the neck and attach this to the head with masking tape. Then tear some more newspaper into small pieces. In a bowl, add water to PVA glue to thin it a little, dip the torn pieces into it and apply to the head and neck, covering them completely and ensuring that the surface is smooth. Leave to dry for several hours.

tip

Use gouache paints rather than poster paints for the angel's head because these are much easier to paint over if you need to cover a mistake. A final layer of paper varnish or undiluted PVA glue gives a nice shiny finish, and also protects the paint.

3 Paint the head with flesh-coloured paint and add eyes, nose, lips and cheeks. Leave to dry. Cut five 15cm (6in.) lengths of ric rac for hair, and glue on to the head.

4 Apply glue around the neck and press the dress to it until it is firmly attached. Leave to dry. Glue little sequins around the bottom of the skirt.

5 Make five loops with the wire tinsel, using about 17cm (7in.) of tinsel for each one. Then make five smaller loops using about 11cm (4½in.) for each one. Fix the tinsel to the angel's back, leaving enough to twist around a branch to fasten the angel to the tree. Glue velvet ribbon around the neck. Then make a small tinsel tiara and glue in place.

papier-maché angel

❄ ❄

MATERIALS

Paper for pattern and template on page 91

White fabric

Pins and scissors

Needle and thread

Stuffing

Newspaper

PVA glue, bowl and water

White paint and paintbrush

Lustre powder in white and copper/gold

Gouache paints for flesh, hair and features

About 20cm (8in.) of thin gold ribbon

Silver wire for the tie

The smoothness of this charming angel comes from using small pieces of paper. Lustre powders give a beautifully pearly finish but you can use ordinary gouache paint instead, and sprinkle fine glitter on to the surface while the paint is still wet.

1 Using the template on page 91, make paper patterns for the angel's body, wings and arms. Fold the fabric in half, pin the pattern pieces in place and cut out two body pieces, two wing pieces and two pieces for each arm.

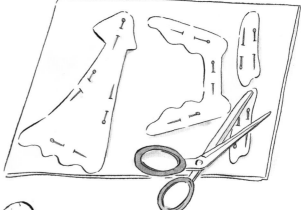

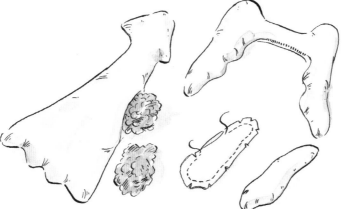

2 With right sides facing, stitch together the body pieces, and then the wings and arms, leaving a small opening on each. Snip any curved seam allowances (to allow the material to lie flat) and turn the pieces right side out. Insert the stuffing, pushing it into all corners, and hand stitch the openings closed.

3 In a bowl, add some water to the PVA glue to thin it slightly. Tear newspaper into small pieces, dip these in the glue and smooth them on to the padded shapes, using the smaller pieces around the edges and shaped areas. Apply two layers of newspaper and leave to dry overnight. Then paint the body, wings and arms with white paint so that the newsprint does not show through. Leave to dry.

4 Mix the white lustre powder with a little PVA, paint on to the body and arms and leave to dry. Mix the copper/gold lustre powder with some PVA and paint on to the wings. Paint the hair, face and features and hands with the gouache paints.

5 Tie gold ribbon round the angel's neck and glue the arms and wings in place. Twist silver wire around the middle of the wings to use to fasten the angel to the tree.

organza fairy

❄ ❄

MATERIALS

Paper for the pattern and template on page 91

Pins and scissors

Needle and thread

Cream cotton fabric

Stuffing

Metallic organza

Fast-drying craft glue

Fine sequins

Large shiny sequins

Embroidery thread in green, red, pink and brown

75cm (30in.) length of 4cm (1½in.) wide organza ribbon

Glitter and glue

Scrap of ribbon for hair bow

40cm (16in.) length of 15mm (½in.) wide velvet ribbon

A beautiful ball gown covers this glamorous fairy's simple fabric body, and she is bedecked with sequins, large and small. A pretty shawl and little glitter shoes complete the look.

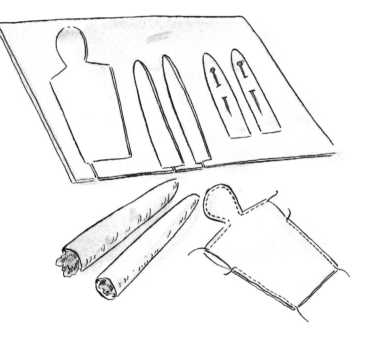

1 Using the templates on page 91, make paper patterns, pin to the cream cotton fabric and cut out two body shapes, four leg shapes and four arm shapes. With right sides facing, machine stitch the arms and legs, leaving the tops open. Snip curved seams (to allow material to lie flat) and turn right way out.

Stitch the two body pieces together around the head and shoulders and down each side leaving the bottom open and a 2cm (³⁄₄in.) gap for each arm at either side. Stuff the arms and the legs.

2 Turn the body the right way out and push the arms in position, turning in 1cm (½in.) at each opening on the body. Stitch the arms in place and stuff the body. Tack the legs in position and stitch the bottom of the body closed.

3 Cut a 13 x 7cm (5 x 2¾in.) piece of organza. Fold lengthways and glue around the torso of the doll, holding in place until well fixed.

4 Cut two rectangles of organza 14 x 45cm (5½ x 17¾in.). Sew running stitch along the top edge of each piece and gather to form a skirt. Hold the gathers in place with a few stitches at the end. Glue one of the skirts in place on the doll. Then glue a line of small sequins along the bottom of the second skirt and when the glue is dry, glue this over the first skirt around the doll.

5 Glue shiny sequins around the waist and neckline of the dress, holding in place until securely fixed. Stitch two french knots on to the face for eyes in green embroidery thread, a small stitch of pink thread for the nose and a few small stitches of red thread to form the mouth. Finish off the stitches at the back of the head.

6 Glue 1cm (½in.) lengths of brown embroidery thread to the head to form a fringe. For the rest of the hair, cut longer lengths, about 9cm (3½in.), and glue them over the head from one side to the other. When the glue is dry, trim the hair to the required length. Glue a thin strip of sequins around the fairy's neck for a necklace.

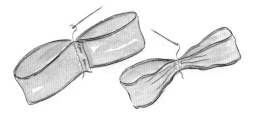

7 With 40cm (16in.) of organza ribbon, make a loop, overlapping the ends of the ribbon slightly, and stitch together. Using running stitch, sew one side of the ribbon to the other to form two equal loops, and gather slightly. Do the same with a 35cm (14in.) length of ribbon. Stitch both pieces to the back of the fairy to form wings.

8 Cut a piece of organza 22 x 5cm (9 x 2in.) and glue sequins along both ends. Wrap this around the fairy's shoulders, like a shawl, and stitch in place. Paint glue on the end of the legs and sprinkle with glitter to make sparkly shoes. Leave to dry. Make a bow from a scrap of fabric and glue to the side of the head. Then sew the velvet ribbon to the fairy's back, just below the wings, to tie her to the tree.

knitted fairy

MATERIALS

Knitting needles (size 3)

Pale pink wool

Cream wool

Needle and thread

Stuffing

Yellow wool

2 small blue beads

Pink embroidery thread

Silver embroidery thread

Silver ric rac

Fast-drying craft glue

Silver ribbon

Thin ribbon

Only the most basic knowledge of knitting is necessary to make this cuddly fairy. Great for children, she would look lovely on a tree decorated with home-made woolly pompom baubles.

1 Using pink wool, cast on 20 stitches and knit stocking stitch for 20 rows. Change to cream wool and knit another 25 rows. Cast off.

2 Fold the knitted panel lengthways and, using cream wool, stitch up the sides. With the seam at centre back, sew running stitch around the top of the head section (pink) and gather. Finish with a few stitches to hold in place. Fill the knitted body with stuffing and stitch closed.

3 Tie a strand of pink wool around the body, about 4cm (1½in.) from the top, and pull in gently to make the head. Knot at the back and trim the ends of the wool.

tip

This fairy sits well on a small tree. To make an angel for a bigger tree, increase the length of the skirt piece by adding on rows, keeping the head and arms the same size. For a fuller skirt, cast on more stitches to make the piece wider and gather up in the same way as step 5.

4 Stitch some lengths of yellow wool to the top of the head to form the hair, sew on small beads for eyes and sew a small mouth with pink embroidery thread.

5 Using the same knitting needles, and cream wool, cast on 60 stitches and knit stocking stitch to a length of about 10cm (4in.). Cast off. Sew running stitch along the top of the knitting and gather to make the fairy's skirt. Embroider with stars, using the silver thread. Stitch the skirt on to the body and glue silver ric rac around the top. Glue a length of ric rac to the head to make a crown.

6 For the arms, cast on 8 stitches in cream wool and knit a 10cm (4in.) panel in stocking stitch. Cast off. Using cream wool, stitch the knitted panel lengthways to form a roll, and sew each end to either side of the body. Tie two pieces of silver ribbon into bows, one slightly bigger than the other, and sew to the back of the fairy, the bigger one on top, to make the wings. Then, under these, stitch a length of thin ribbon to make a tie.

ric rac fairy

❄ ❄

MATERIALS

Cream fabric for head

Green spotted fabric
for body

Blue spotted fabric
for skirt

Scissors

Needle and thread

Paper for pattern and
template on page 92

Pins

Stuffing

60cm (24in.) of 8mm
(¼in.) wide
gingham ribbon

35cm (14in.) blue ric rac

25cm (10in.) pink
bobble fringe

Fast-drying craft glue

Blue and pink embroidery
thread and needle

1 metre (40in.) gold ric rac
for hair

Scrap of white ric rac
for crown

Button for crown and two
for feet

Perfect for a less formal tree, this cute fairy is made from scraps of fabric and buttons. Stitch the body and then raid your workbox for bits of ric rac, braid and buttons to decorate her. Gingham ribbon stitched to her back forms her wings when tied to the tree.

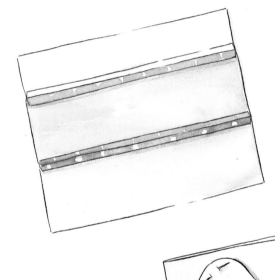

1 Cut a piece of cream fabric measuring 6 x 26cm (2¼ x 10¼in.), a piece of body fabric 9 x 26cm (3½ x 10¼in.) and a piece of skirt fabric 9.5 x 26cm (3¾ x 10¼in.). With right sides facing, sew the long sides of the cream fabric and body fabric together, and then the long sides of the body and skirt fabric. Press the seams open.

2 Cut out a paper pattern for the fairy using the template on page 92. Fold the fabric panel in half and lay the paper pattern across it as shown. Pin and cut out.

tip

To simplify this fairy, cut out the front and back from one piece of fabric rather than joining bands of different fabrics as here. Make the face with buttons so that the features stand out.

3 With right sides facing, pin and stitch the two pieces together, leaving the bottom open. Turn right side out and fill with stuffing. Turn in the raw bottom edge by 1.5cm (½in.). Cut two pieces of gingham ribbon, each 5cm (2in.) long, position them inside the bottom open edge to form legs and tack in place. Then stitch along the bottom.

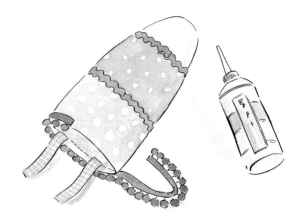

4 Glue ric rac around the neck and waist of the fairy, overlapping the ends at the back, and then glue a length of bobble fringe around the bottom, again overlapping the ends at the back.

5 Embroider two blue French knots on the face for eyes and make a few small pink stitches to form the mouth. Finish with a few stitches at the back of the head. Cut eight 12.5cm (5in.) lengths of gold ric rac and glue around the head to make the hair.

6 Glue a piece of ric rac on to the head to make a crown and decorate with a button glued to the middle. Glue a button on to each leg. Stitch a length of gingham ribbon to the back of the fairy, at its centre, and tie to the tree with a large bow to form the wings.

peg-doll fairy

❄ ❄

MATERIALS

Wooden peg

Selection of gouache paints for the skin, hair and features

Paintbrush

Gold organza

Scissors, needle and thread

Fast-drying, high tack craft glue

60cm (24in.) of 35mm (1½in.) wide gold organza ribbon

Flower sequin for hair

Star sequin and string of tiny sequins for the wand

Gold sequins

Ribbon about 40cm (16in.) long

Add a touch of sophistication to your tree with this beautiful Christmas fairy. No one will guess that she is made from a plain, old-fashioned wooden peg 'dressed' with organza and sequins.

1 Paint the peg with flesh-coloured paint. When dry, paint the hair and facial features. Again leave to dry.

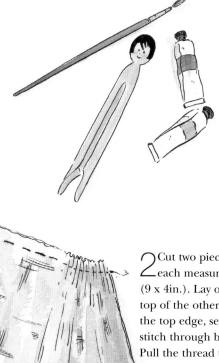

2 Cut two pieces of organza, each measuring 22 x 10cm (9 x 4in.). Lay one piece on top of the other and, close to the top edge, sew running stitch through both layers. Pull the thread to gather the material, making sure that it fits around the peg. Finish with a few stitches to hold the gathers.

tip

If you cannot find a flower sequin for the fairy's hair decoration, glue a tiny ribbon bow in place instead, or a cluster of tiny beads in a flower shape.

3 Position the skirt around the peg and stitch together at the back. Apply a dab of glue to the peg and skirt to hold in place if necessary.

4 Fold the gold ribbon in half lengthways. Dab glue around the body of the peg and wrap the ribbon around it, tying it at the back. Leave to dry. Open out the remaining ribbon and trim the ends in a V shape.

5 Tie the ribbon in an extravagant bow. Glue a flower sequin to the hair. Make a wand from string sequins and a star sequin, and glue in place. Glue gold sequins on to the skirt. Stitch a ribbon to the back of the fairy for the tie.

button snowflake

❄ ❄

MATERIALS

2 buttons about 30mm
(1in.) in diameter

16 buttons about 22mm
(⁹/₁₀in.) in diameter

16 buttons about 20mm
(⁴/₅in.) in diameter

24 buttons about 17mm
(⁷/₁₀in.) in diameter

16 buttons about 15mm
(³/₅in.) in diameter

16 buttons about 12mm
(¹/₂in.) in diameter

16 buttons about 7mm
(¹/₄in.) in diameter

Glue gun and glue sticks

4 lengths of florist's wire,
each about 25cm (10in.)

Snippers for wire

Scrap paper and pencil

Ruler

40cm (16in.) of 10mm
(¹/₂in.) wide ribbon

Craft knife

Create a beautiful and everlasting decoration for your tree with this unusual snowflake. Mother-of-pearl buttons add an extra special touch but any buttons can be used.

1 Arrange the buttons in order of size. Lay one of the large buttons wrong side up on the work surface and apply a blob of glue just above and just below the holes. This will reduce the amount of glue that oozes through to the front of the button. Press a length of wire on to it so that the button is placed centrally. Stick the next size of button directly above the central button, butting up the edges.

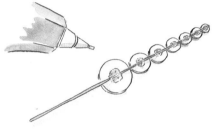

Again, try to apply the glue to either side of the holes. Continue with five more buttons, decreasing in size, and repeat on the other side of the central button.

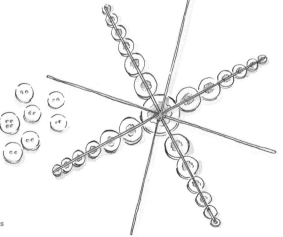

2 Cut another length of wire in half and glue each piece to the central button to form a cross with the first wire. Glue on buttons as before. Lay the cross of buttons face down on a piece of scrap paper, and draw lines to make a star shape. Cut the remaining two lengths of wire in half.

3 Using the drawn lines as guides, lay 17mm (⁷/₁₀in.) buttons next to the central button, in the gaps. Then, continue along each drawn arm, first with a slightly bigger button followed by smaller ones, decreasing in size as before. Glue the wires to the backs of the buttons, and to the central button. Then glue all the corresponding buttons on to the backs of the snowflake buttons apart from the central button.

4 Lay the ribbon across the back of the star, make sure it's taut and flat, and glue to the central button. Glue the remaining big button in place. To remove any excess glue from the buttons, carefully scrape off with a craft knife making sure that the buttons themselves do not get scratched.

pearl bead snowflake

❄ ❄

MATERIALS

Silver jeweller's wire

Pliers

Selection of pearly beads

Glue gun and glue sticks

Length of florist's wire

This charming snowflake is so beautiful it may well become a family heirloom. Beads in lovely pearly colours are threaded on to stiff wire and glued in place.

1 Cut three lengths of silver jeweller's wire, each measuring 30cm (12in.). Thread five beads of varying sizes on to each one and thread the same pattern of beads in reverse on the other end.

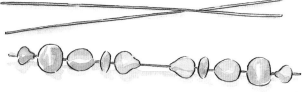

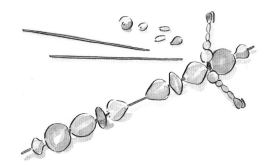

2 Cut another three lengths, this time 15cm (6in.) long, and twist each one to the existing arms between the second and third beads. Thread five beads on to each side of these short arms and bend the ends of the wires over the end beads, trimming if necessary. Apply a small dab of glue to the main arm's last bead and wire.

3 Lay the three long beaded lengths on top of each other and twist them together at the centre to hold them in place.

tip
If using large beads,
the snowflake may
become quite heavy
and will be more suited
to a larger tree that will
support the weight.

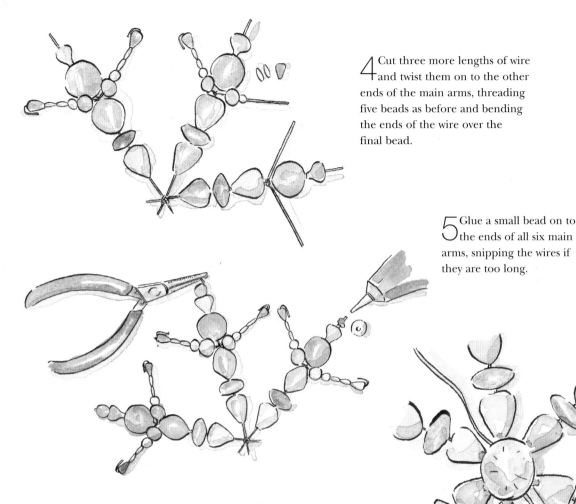

4 Cut three more lengths of wire and twist them on to the other ends of the main arms, threading five beads as before and bending the ends of the wire over the final bead.

5 Glue a small bead on to the ends of all six main arms, snipping the wires if they are too long.

6 Twist a length of thick florist's wire around the centre of the snowflake and push to the back to attach to the top of the tree. With the glue gun, glue a bead to the centre of the snowflake to finish it.

clear seed bead snowflake

MATERIALS

Silver jeweller's wire

Pliers

Clear seed beads

Clear bugle beads

This delicate snowflake will add subtle elegance to your festive decorations. Clear beads catch the light beautifully, so drape fairy lights around the top of the tree to make the snowflake glisten.

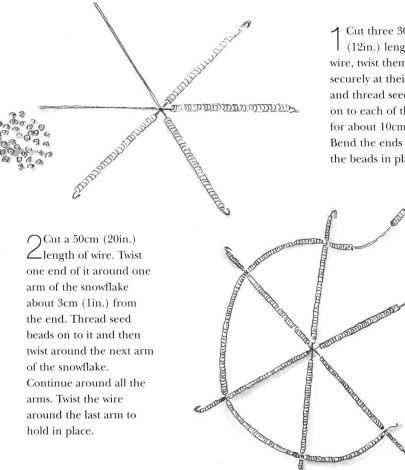

1 Cut three 30cm (12in.) lengths of wire, twist them together securely at their centres and thread seed beads on to each of the six arms for about 10cm (4in.). Bend the ends to keep the beads in place.

2 Cut a 50cm (20in.) length of wire. Twist one end of it around one arm of the snowflake about 3cm (1in.) from the end. Thread seed beads on to it and then twist around the next arm of the snowflake. Continue around all the arms. Twist the wire around the last arm to hold in place.

3 Cut six 15cm (6in.) lengths of wire. Take one and twist one end to an arm just above the circle of beads and thread on three bugle beads, then seven seed beads and another three bugle beads and form a petal shape. Twist the wire around the main arm and repeat to make another petal on the other side. Twist around the main arm again and trim. Repeat on each arm of the snowflake.

4 Cut a 120cm (47in.) length of wire. Twist one end of it on to a main arm about 8cm (3in.) from the end. Thread on six bugle beads and twist around the next arm. When the circle is complete, thread two bugle beads on to the wire, three seed beads and another two bugle beads, and twist around the main arm. Thread on three bugle beads, seven seed beads and another three bugle beads and form a petal shape. Twist around the wire circle and thread two bugle, three seed and two bugle beads, forming another petal. Repeat all the way round.

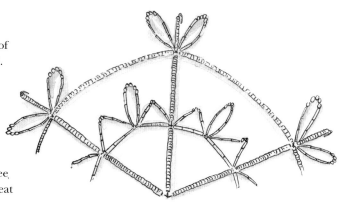

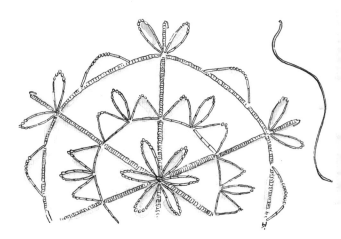

5 For the flower shape at the centre of the snowflake, cut six lengths of wire. On each one, thread three bugle beads, seven seed beads and another three bugle beads and twist the wire ends around the centre.

6 Cut another six lengths of wire and thread with two bugle beads, seven seed beads and another two bugle beads. Twist these on to the outer circle of the snowflake, one in each section. Twist more wire around the centre a couple of times to attach the snowflake to the tree.

pipe cleaner snowflake

❄ ❄

MATERIALS

14 white pipe cleaners, each 30cm (12in.) long

Scissors

Silver jeweller's wire

Newspaper

Spray adhesive

White glitter

With a few twists and turns, this crisp snowflake takes shape. Finished with a light sprinkle of white glitter to create a subtle shimmer, it stands out against the background of a Christmas tree.

1 Using four of the pipe cleaners, twist each end to form a loop about 2cm (³/₄in.) long, bending the end of the wire round the main stem to hold in place.

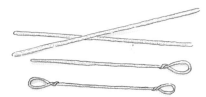

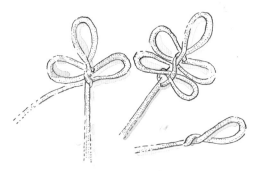

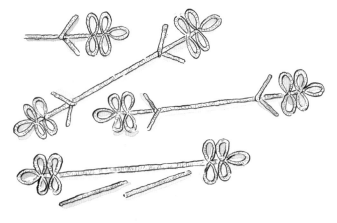

2 Take another pipe cleaner and twist the end underneath the loop of one of the pipe cleaners from step 1 to form a loop at each side. Bend the pipe cleaner round the main stem and make another two loops underneath the first, finishing by twisting the pipe cleaner round the main stem and trimming off any excess with a pair of scissors. Repeat at the ends of all four pipe cleaners.

3 Cut eight pieces of pipe cleaner measuring 7cm (2³/₄in.). Twist them on to each pipe cleaner about 8cm (3in.) from the end and form into V shapes.

4 Lay the four pipe cleaners across each other to make a snowflake shape. Cut a piece of wire about 20cm (8in.) long and bind around the centre of the snowflake to hold all the pipe cleaners together. The end of the wire should be at the back of the snowflake, so that it can be used as a tie. In a well-ventilated area, and having covered the work surface with newspaper, spray the snowflake with spray adhesive, sprinkle it with white glitter and shake off any excess.

shiny bead snowflake

MATERIALS

Silver jeweller's wire

Selection of metallic and pearly beads

Pliers

Metallic beads have a delightfully frosted look that works perfectly for this stylish decoration. The beads are threaded on to wire with smaller 'arms' added to make the shape of the snowflake, using beads in shades of green and silver.

1 Cut three lengths of wire, each measuring 30cm (12in.). Thread beads on to each wire for about 10cm (4in.), starting with four small ones. Then thread on the same pattern of beads in reverse. Bend the ends of the wire slightly to keep the beads in place. Leave some space between the beads at this stage.

2 Lay the three beaded wires on top of each other to form a star shape and twist them together at their centres to hold them in place.

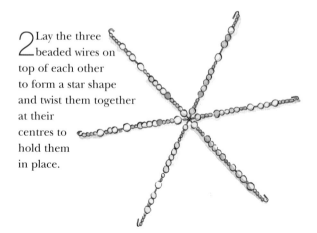

3 Cut another three lengths of wire measuring 15cm (6in.). Thread beads on to them as before, this time for about 5cm (2in.), and again repeat the bead pattern in reverse, leaving some space between the beads and bending over the ends of the wire slightly. Twist the short lengths of beaded wire evenly around the centre of the star shape.

tip
Before you start, make
sure the wire is narrow
enough to thread through
the beads.

4 Cut six lengths of wire measuring 7cm (2¾in.) each. Twist them on to the short beaded lengths just underneath the end bead. Thread small beads on to each arm of the wire for about 2cm (¾in.) and trim the ends. Bend the wire over the last bead to hold in place. Do the same on all the short lengths.

5 Cut six lengths of wire measuring 10cm (4in.). Twist them on to the long beaded lengths about 4cm (1½in.) from the end and thread beads on to both arms for about 3.5cm (1½in.). Trim the ends of the wire and bend over the end bead. Push all the beads close together and re-trim the wire, making sure the ends are bent over the last beads. Twist about 30cm (12in.) of wire around the middle of the snowflake, push through to the back and use this to fasten the snowflake to the tree.

pine-cone star

❊ ❊

MATERIALS

1 large pine cone

18 small pine cones

Florist's wire and pliers

PVA glue and paintbrush

Newspaper

White glitter

Take inspiration from nature with this lovely star. A light dusting of glitter gives the cones a beautiful frosted finish.

1 Take a length of wire and push through the lower part of a small pine cone. Twist the wire round it to hold securely. Add another pine cone, twisting the wire around it again and then add a third. Make six of these three-cone wires.

2 Push the ends of the wires through the lower section of the large pine cone and twist round to hold each arm in place, arranging them evenly.

3 Paint PVA glue on to the pine cones, dabbing it roughly over them. Lay the star on newspaper and sprinkle glitter all over it. Shake off any excess and leave to dry.

4 Twist a length of wire around the underside of the large pine cone, fastening it securely to attach the star to the tree top.

tip
This star is very
economical to make if
you gather the pine
cones from parks and
woods, where they have
fallen from the trees.

glitter star

✳ ✳

MATERIALS

Paper for pattern and
templates on page 93

Thin card

Pencil, ruler and craft knife

Cutting mat or scrap paper

Fast-drying craft glue

Glitter

Cardboard cut into a star shape, scored with a craft knife and
then gently folded creates a simple 3-D decoration. Cover it
with fine glitter for a stylish tree topper.

1 Using the template on page 93, a pencil,
ruler and craft knife, draw and cut
out a star shape from thin card.
A cutting mat or pile of scrap paper will
protect the work surface.

2 Score lines from point to point on the
star by gently pulling the craft knife
along the edge of the ruler to cut just the
surface of the card. Do not press too hard
or the knife will cut through the card.
Follow all the lines as indicated on the
template, and gently bend the card to give
it shape.

3 Using the other
template, cut out a
piece of card for the
base and roll it into a
cone shape. Glue the
edges together,
holding it in place
until the glue has
dried slightly.

4 Paint the star and base with glue,
ensuring an even finish. Sprinkle
glitter all over it and shake gently to
remove any excess. Leave to dry.

tip
Glitter is available in lots
of different colours so
your star doesn't have to
be silver. Make a star
using coloured glitter to
co-ordinate with the
other decorations.

organza star

❋ ❋

MATERIALS

Organza

Needle and thread

Stuffing

Fast-drying craft glue

String of sequins

Little sparkly jewels

Gold ric rac

Wide organza ribbon

This bejewelled fabric star will take pride of place at the top of the Christmas tree. Tie it on with a sumptuous bow, ensuring the sparkly star looks equally lovely from front and back.

1 Using the template on page 93, cut out two stars from organza. With wrong sides facing, sew the two together with running stitch all the way round, leaving an opening along one point of the star.

2 Fill the star with stuffing, making sure that the stuffing is pushed into the points and there are no lumps. Stitch the opening closed.

3 Apply a thin line of glue all round the star close to the edge and press sequins to it. Overlap the ends slightly and leave the glue to dry for a few minutes.

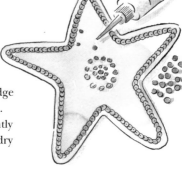

4 Decorate the star by applying small dabs of glue to it and carefully sticking on little sparkly jewels.

5 Apply glue all round the edge of the star and run ric rac along it, holding it in place until it is fixed. Overlap the ends slightly.

6 Cut a length of organza ribbon long enough to tie in a bow and stitch it to the back of the star. Use this to tie the star to the tree.

ribbon poinsettia

MATERIALS

110cm (43in.) of 6.5cm (2½in.) wide red wired taffeta ribbon

75cm (30in.) of 6.5cm (2½in.) green wired taffeta ribbon

20cm (8in.) of 2.5cm (1in.) wide red wired taffeta ribbon

Scissors, needle and thread

Green metallic beads

40cm (16in.) of 22mm (¾in.) wide red satin ribbon

This red flower is the perfect tree-top decoration. Wired ribbon holds its shape, and taffeta gives a lovely sheen.

1 Cut six 9cm (3½in.) lengths of the wide red ribbon. Sew small running stitches at both ends of each strip and pull up so that the ribbon is gathered, securing it with a few stitches. Stitch the ends of three petals together and then do the same with the other three. Stitch the two sets of three together at the centre to form an even flower. Then cut six 8cm (3in.) lengths of the same wide red ribbon and repeat to make a slightly smaller flower.

2 Cut four 10cm (4in.) lengths of green ribbon, sew running stitches at one end of each and gather as before. Cut the other end of each strip into a leaf shape.

3 Stitch the leaves to the back of the smaller flower at regular intervals. Then stitch the large flower to the back of this. Cut a 30cm (12in.) length of green ribbon, fold it in half and stitch to the back of the flower, cutting a neat V shape in both ends.

4 Cut two lengths of the thinner taffeta ribbon and sew a few stitches in the centre of each one to gather them slightly. Cut the ends into petal shapes and stitch the ribbon petals crossways in the middle of the flower. Finish with a few beads at the centre. Stitch a length of satin ribbon to the back of the flower to make a tie, and if necessary, adjust the petals and leaves to sit evenly.

patterned fabric flower

✱✲✳✱✲✳✱✲✳✱✲✳✱✲✳✱✲✳✱✲✳✱✲✳✱✲✳✱✲✳✱✲✳✱✲✳✱✲✳

MATERIALS

3 different patterns of red fabrics

Paper for pattern and template on page 90

Self-covering button with spotty fabric

40cm (16in.) of red ribbon

Go dotty for this cute spotty flower. Polka-dot fabric with its endearingly retro feel creates a jolly bloom, but any fabric could be used. Co-ordinate other tree decorations to match, choosing strong shapes in keeping with the tree topper.

1 Using the template on page 90, cut out patterns for the two sizes of petals. Then cut out two times eight of the bigger petals in the same fabric. With right sides facing, pin and machine stitch each one, leaving the end open. Make small snips round the seam allowance (so that the material lies flat), turn right side out and press. Using the smaller petal pattern, make three petals as before in each of the other two fabrics, and press.

2 Gather the open end of each of the bigger petals slightly and hold in place with a few stitches. Then stitch the petals together to form a flower.

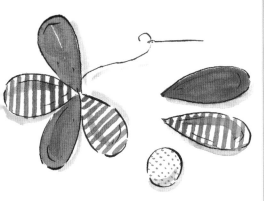

3 Repeat step 2 using the smaller petals, alternating the two fabric patterns. Stitch to the middle of the big flower and sew the button to the centre.

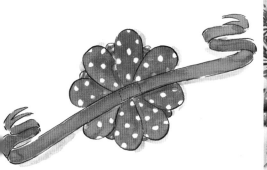

4 Stitch the ribbon to the back of the flower securely to make the tie.

metallic foil flowers tied in a bunch

MATERIALS

Paper for pattern and templates on page 92

Metallic foil

Scissors

Scrap paper

Ballpoint pen

Pin

Thin silver wire

Pliers

Small metallic beads

Glue gun and sticks

40cm (16in.) of wired ribbon

This bouquet adds a subtle, elegant charm to your tree. The sparkling metallic flowers are arranged by bending the silver-wire stems to make a stunning display.

1 Using the templates on page 92, make two paper patterns for the flowers and cut out six large and four small flowers from the foil.

2 Place the foil flowers on a pile of scrap paper and, using the ballpoint pen, make small dots all the way round the petals, a line from the centre along each petal and a few dots around the middle.

3 Using a pin, make a small hole at the centre of each flower. Cut about 25cm (10in.) of silver wire and push this through the hole from back to front. Thread a bead on to the wire and push the wire back through the hole.

tip

Metallic foils are available in copper and
gold as well as silver. Flowers in these
lovely finishes would make a very pretty
display. Alternatively, glass paint, which
is available in a wide selection of hues,
can be applied to silver foil to create
flowers in all sorts of colours for a
beautifully bright bouquet.

4 Twist the wire around itself at the back of the flower. Apply a little glue to the back of the flower, using the glue gun, and stick the wire down.

6 Tie the ribbon around the bunch and to the top of the tree, finishing with a neat bow. Trim the ends of the ribbon if necessary.

5 When all the flowers have been wired, make a bunch and twist the wires together to hold in place. Trim the ends of the wire so that they are all the same length.

beaded berries

❄ ❄

MATERIALS

Green jeweller's wire

Red seed beads

Green seed beads

Fast-drying craft glue

12 beads for the berries

Length of florist's wire

Wire cutters

Ribbon

Red berries are a traditional motif at Christmas time, and these beautiful beaded berries, gathered in a leafy cluster and tied on to the tree, will keep their shape and colour perfectly throughout the holiday season.

1 Cut a 20cm (8in.) length of jeweller's wire and thread a bead on to the end of it. Bend the wire over the bead and twist the end back on itself to hold it in place. Paint the bead with glue and sprinkle red seed beads on to it to cover it completely. Make 12 of these.

3 Continue to wire the beaded berries on to the main stem, varying the angles and making the stems of the berries gradually longer towards the bottom.

2 Take a length of florist's wire and start to twist the berry stems on to it, making sure that they are firmly held in place. Snip off any excess wire.

4 Cut a 15cm (6in.) length of green wire and thread green seed beads on to the end. Bend the beaded section into a leaf shape and then twist the end of it around the rest of the wire at the base of the leaf to keep the beads in place. Make several of these leaves.

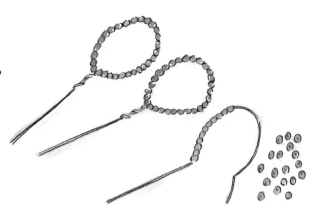

6 Cut a 20cm (8in.) length of green wire and thread green seed beads on to it, bending both ends so that the beads stay in place. Twist it on to the main stem of the berry cluster to form the bottom of the bunch. Cut a length of ribbon and tie the cluster in place on the tree with it, finishing with a bow.

5 Attach the leaves to the berry cluster by twisting the ends on to the main stem as before. Vary the angles of the leaves and twist the stems around until you are happy with the arrangement.

glitter bird

✳ ✳

MATERIALS

Paper for pattern and template on page 90

25cm (10in.) length of 135cm (53in.) wide velvet fabric

Pins

Scissors

Needle and thread

Feathers

Stuffing

Seed beads

Sequins

Flower sequin

Bugle beads

50cm (20in.) of 15mm (½in.) wide velvet ribbon

A sparkling blue velvet bird with a delicate feathery tail and sequinned wings looks fabulous perched on the top of a traditional Christmas tree, or clipped to your own resplendent arrangement of branches and twigs.

1 Make a paper pattern using the template on page 90, pin to the velvet fabric and cut out two pieces for the bird's body, one piece for the base and two wing pieces.

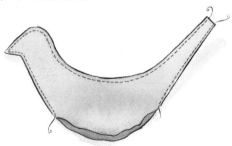

2 With right sides facing, pin and stitch the two body pieces together, leaving a gap of 12cm (4¾in.) at the bottom and a gap at the tail.

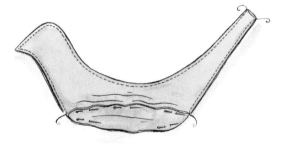

3 Pin the base piece along the opening at the bottom of the bird, leaving a gap of about 4cm (1½in.) along one side. Turn right side out.

4 Turn in the raw edge at the tail by 1.5cm (½in.) and push the base of the feathers into it. Hand stitch securely in place.

5 Fill the bird with small pieces of stuffing, pushing them through the opening right into the beak and tail shape. Make sure that there are no lumps and when the bird is full, hand stitch the opening closed.

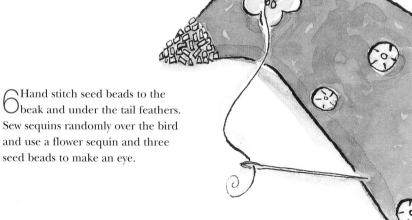

6 Hand stitch seed beads to the beak and under the tail feathers. Sew sequins randomly over the bird and use a flower sequin and three seed beads to make an eye.

7 Take the two velvet wing pieces and, right sides facing, pin and stitch them together, leaving an opening of about 2.5cm (1in.) along one edge. Snip around the seam allowance and turn right side out. Hand stitch the opening closed and press.

8 Decorate the wings with bugle beads and seed beads and hand stitch them on to the body of the bird. Stitch the velvet ribbon to the back of the bird securely to make the tie.

organza butterfly

MATERIALS

50cm (20in.) of silver jeweller's wire

Small silver beads

10 beads about 7mm (¼in.) wide

4 glass beads for antennae

Pliers

Scissors, needle and thread

Copper-coloured organza 25cm (10in.)

String sequins 1 metre (40in.)

String of small sequins 50cm (20in.)

Selection of sequins

Fast-drying, high tack glue

40cm (16in.) of 36mm (1½in.) wide gold organza ribbon

This delicate butterfly looks as though it has just landed on the tree. Its body and antennae are beaded while its wings are strips of shimmery organza. Make smaller butterflies in the same way to decorate the rest of the tree, adding sequins for extra twinkle.

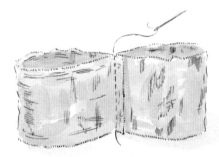

1 Fold the wire in two and thread one small silver bead on to it, pushing the bead to the bend. Thread the other beads on to the two strands of wire together, alternating between small silver beads and larger ones.

2 Pull the ends of the wire slightly apart to form antennae, and thread a glass bead on to each one. Follow these with 12 small silver beads and finish with another glass bead on both pieces of wire. Trim the wire and bend the end over the glass bead to hold securely in place.

3 Cut a piece of organza measuring 45 x 10cm (17¾ x 4in.). Fray the edges. Fold the strip in half lengthways. Overlap the ends slightly and join one side to the other in the middle, using running stitch through all the layers. Pull the thread to gather and secure with a few stitches.

4 Cut another piece of organza measuring 40 x 6cm (16 x 2¼in.) and repeat step 3. Lay both sets of wings on to a work surface with the join facing down and lay the bead body centrally on to them. Stitch the wings on to the body and fasten securely in place.

5 Cut several lengths of sequins and glue on to the wings. Finish the butterfly with loose sequins glued around the wings and leave to dry.

6 Stitch the centre of the gold ribbon to the back of the butterfly to make a tie.

grosgrain ribbon rosette

❋ ❋

MATERIALS

105 x 8cm (41½ x 3in.) grosgrain ribbon, salmon pink

Needle and thread

Fast-drying craft glue

56 x 5cm (22 x 2in.) grosgrain ribbon, shocking pink

90 x 2.5cm (35½ x 1in.) grosgrain ribbon, orange

30mm (1¼in.) button

Make a statement with this bold, contemporary ribbon rosette. Grosgrain ribbon holds its shape very well and falls easily into neat folds, so is perfect for making this striking tree decoration.

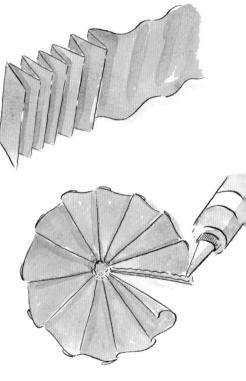

1 Take the salmon pink ribbon and fold it approximately every 5cm (2in.) into a concertina, finishing with both ends facing the same way. Hold the folded ribbon firmly as you go.

2 Carefully push a needle and thread through all the layers of ribbon, centrally and about 5mm (¼in.) from the bottom edge. You may need to separate the layers slightly with your fingers and push the needle through a few layers at a time. Tie the ends of the thread together in front of the raw edges. Knot firmly, close to the ribbon.

3 Apply a line of glue along one raw edge and press against the other raw edge, holding them together until they are firmly stuck.

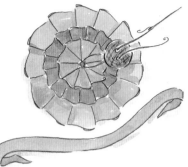

4 Flatten out the rosette, so that the folds are even. Repeat this process with the shocking pink ribbon, folding it about every 3cm (1¼in.), and then with 40cm (16in.) of the orange ribbon, folding it every 2.5cm (1in.). Position the shocking pink rosette centrally on the salmon pink rosette and the orange rosette centrally on these two. Stitch them all in place and sew a button securely to the centre of the rosette. The remaining orange ribbon can be used for the tie. Lay it across the back of the rosette so that an equal length extends each side and stitch it on securely.

taffeta ribbon bow

✳ ✳

MATERIALS

260 x 5cm (102 x 2in.) wired taffeta ribbon

Scissors, needle and thread

30mm (1in.) self-covering button

40 x 1cm (16 x ½in.) satin ribbon for the tie

Presents aren't the only things that can be decorated with a ribbon bow. This smart rosette is made with wired taffeta ribbon fashioned into loops, which can be arranged evenly on the tree.

1 Cut four 45cm (17¾in.) lengths of taffeta ribbon. Form a loop with each piece of ribbon, overlapping the ends by 3cm (1in.). Stitch in place.

2 For each one, flatten the loop, with the join in the middle, and stitch through the layers, pulling the thread to gather the ribbon slightly. With the joins at the back, lay one ribbon loop diagonally across another one, stitching them through the centre to hold the two together. Lay the remaining two loops across diagonally to complete the flower shape, and again stitch each one at the centre to hold in place.

3 Cut a 30cm (12in.) length of the same ribbon. Sew running stitch along one edge and pull the thread to gather the ribbon into a rosette. Finish with a few stitches to secure. Cover a button with a piece of the ribbon, stitch it centrally on to the rosette and then sew this at the centre of the ribbon flower.

4 Cut approximately 40cm (16in.) of the same ribbon and fold in half widthways. Stitch it to the back of the decoration, leaving the ends hanging down, and trim the ends into a V shape. Sew on the satin ribbon just above this to form the tie.

foil heart

MATERIALS

Paper for pattern, template on page 92 and pencil

Metallic foil

Masking tape

Pile of scrap paper

Ballpoint pen

Scissors

Rolling pin

Fast-drying, high tack craft glue

Metallic foil is soft, pliable and easy to work with, so this striking heart decoration is simplicity itself to make, even with its intricate pattern of stars and dainty border.

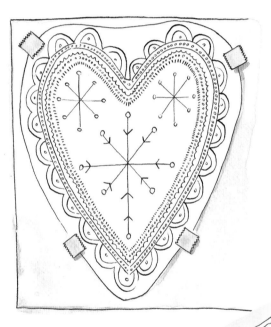

1 Using the template on page 92, make a paper pattern and draw the design on it. Stick this to the foil, using small pieces of masking tape to hold it in place.

2 Lay the foil on a pile of scrap paper with the pattern face up. Draw over the design with the pen, pressing firmly to transfer the pattern to the foil.

tip

Why not decorate the tree with some small
hearts, too? Make them in the same way
as the tree top heart. Use a hole punch to
make a hole at the top of each one, and
hang them on to the branches with lengths
of thin ribbon.

3 Cut out the heart shape from the foil (carefully because the edges of the foil can be sharp). Remove the paper pattern. Go over any areas of pattern that may need it.

4 Lay the cut-out foil on a work surface and roll over it with a rolling pin to flatten it out.

5 Cut an 8 x 12cm (3 x 4¾in.) piece of foil and make this into a roll, using the longer side as the height of the roll. Overlap the edges by about 2cm (¾in.) and glue in place. When the glue is dry, stick the roll to the back of the heart and again leave to dry. This tube will slot over the top branch of the tree and keep the heart in place.

bauble wreath

MATERIALS

Silver wire and cutters

Approximately 55 small baubles between 2cm (³/₄in.) and 2.5cm (1in.) wide in pinks and silver

65 x 3cm (26 x 1¼in.) silver ribbon

Scissors

Wreaths are traditional Christmas decorations so why not use one on the top of the tree? Look for miniature baubles and wire them together to make a mini wreath, finishing it with a ribbon bow.

1 Cut a 150cm (59in.) length of wire. Make a circle with the wire about 13cm (5in.) in diameter, bending it around itself so that it's solid. Then cut as many small pieces of wire as there are baubles. Make them about 10cm (4in.) long, and thread each one through a bauble, twisting the wire firmly.

2 Attach the baubles to the wire circle, winding the wire around to hold the baubles in place securely. Try to avoid using two baubles of the same colour next to each other. Continue attaching baubles to the wire circle until the whole wreath base is covered. Move the baubles if necessary to create an even look.

3 Cut a 35cm (14in.) length of ribbon, and then cut a piece of wire 15cm (6in.) long and twist it around the middle of the ribbon. Push the ends of the wire through the wreath, from the front, and twist to hold it in place at the back.

4 Tie the ribbon in a neat bow and trim the ends at an angle. Tie the rest of the ribbon to the back of the wreath at the top and fasten with a knot. Use this to tie the bauble wreath to the tree.

salt-dough gingerbread man

MATERIALS

Mixing bowl, wooden spoon, measuring jug

150g (5oz) salt

100ml (3½ fl. oz) lukewarm water

150g (5oz) plain flour

½ tablespoon vegetable oil

Rolling pin

Gingerbread cutter

Baking tray

Brown gouache paint and paintbrush

1 metre (40in.) white ric rac

Fast-drying craft glue

2 black buttons

3 white buttons

Small piece of red felt for mouth

25cm (10in.) gingham ribbon for bow

50cm (20in.) ribbon for ties

Strong glue

Make a gingerbread man that looks good enough to eat. Baked hard and then painted, the figure is finished with buttons and ric rac glued around the edge to look like icing.

1 Mix together the salt and water in a bowl, dissolving as much of the salt as possible. Add the flour and oil and mix together to form a pliable dough. Add more water or flour if necessary.

2 Sprinkle flour on to the work surface and roll the dough out to a thickness of about 1.5cm (½in.). Cut the gingerbread man using the cutter and place on the baking tray. Bake in the oven heated to 100C (200F, lowest gas mark setting) for about an hour. Check the dough to see if it is hard. It may need slightly longer – if so, leave in the oven and check regularly. When it's ready, turn off the heat and leave the gingerbread man to cool in the oven to reduce the risk of cracking.

tip

Salt dough is very easy to make and use, but needs to be 'cooked' on a very low temperature so that it does not crack. Leave the salt dough figure in the oven to go completely cold when the oven is turned off to prevent cracking as it cools

3 Paint the figure with brown paint and leave to dry. Paint both sides of the figure ensuring even coverage.

4 Using the fast-drying glue, stick ric rac all the way round the gingerbread man, overlapping the ends slightly. For a neat finish, hold the ric rac in place at corners and curved areas until the glue is dry.

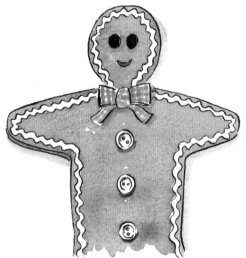

6 Cut two pieces of ribbon, each about 25cm (10in.) long, and use the strong glue to stick them to the back of the gingerbread man, one at the top of the body and the second one slightly lower down. This ensures that the gingerbread man will sit securely at the top of the tree.

5 Glue on black button eyes and red fabric mouth. Stick three white buttons to the middle of the figure, and a gingham bow at the neck. Leave the glue to dry completely.

templates

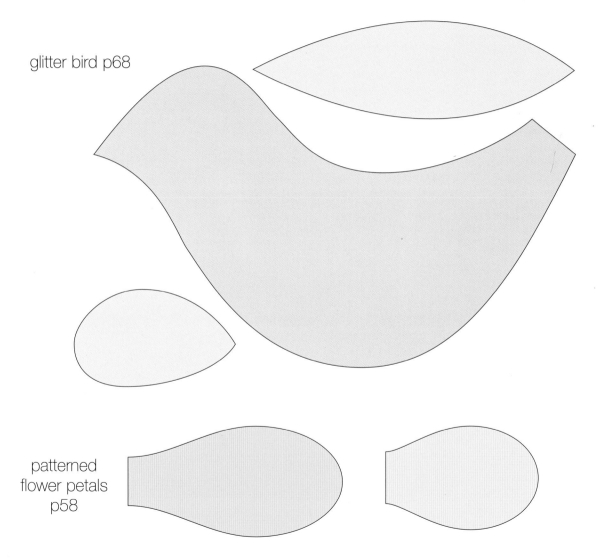

glitter bird p68

patterned
flower petals
p58

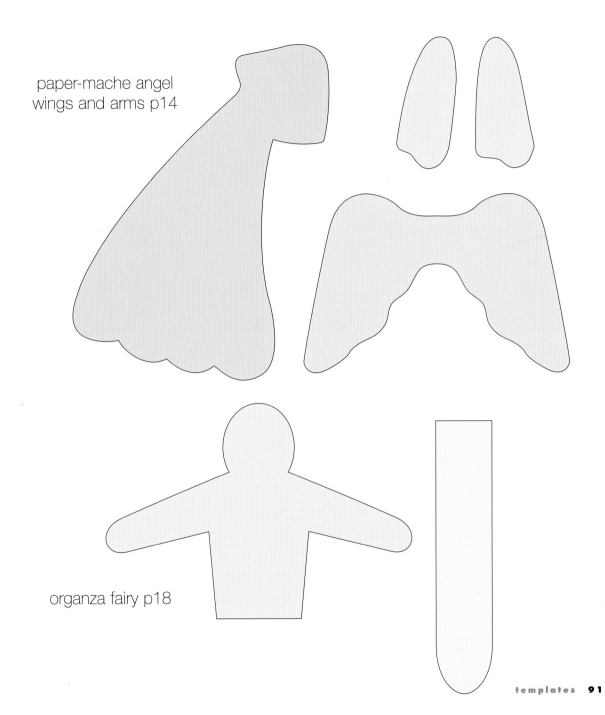

paper-mache angel
wings and arms p14

organza fairy p18

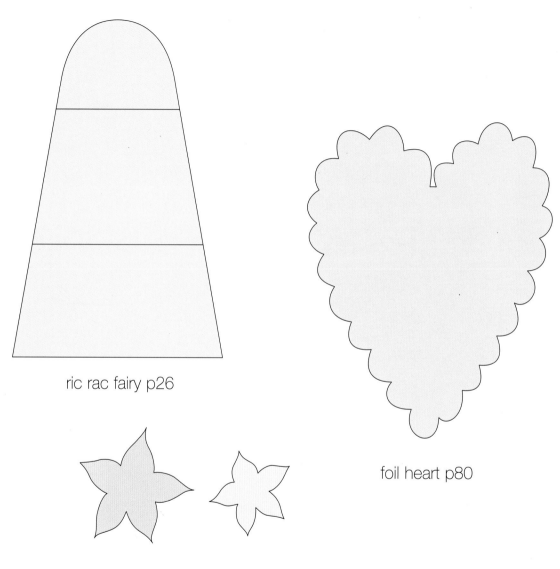

ric rac fairy p26

foil heart p80

foil flowers p60

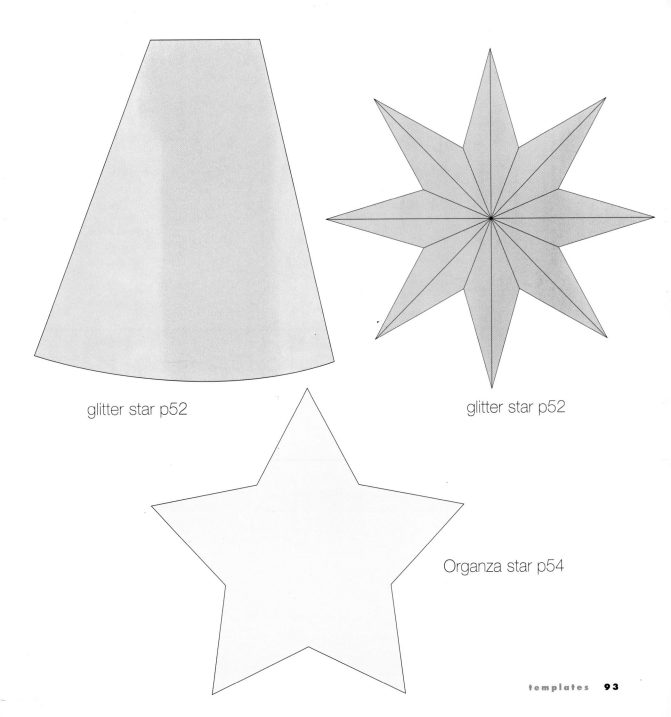

glitter star p52

glitter star p52

Organza star p54

stockists

❄ ❄

The Button Queen,
19 Marylebone Lane,
London W1V 2NF
020 7935 1505
www.thebuttonqueen.co.uk
Great selection of buttons

The Cloth House,
47 Berwick Street,
London W1F 8SJ
020 7437 5155
Good selection of buttons and vintage
trimmings and also at
98 Berwick Street,
London W1F 0QJ
020 7287 1555
www.clothhouse.co.uk
Beautiful selection of organza, velvet and
silk fabrics

L. Cornellisen & Son,
105 Great Russell Street,
London WC1B 3RY
020 7636 1045
www.cornellisen.com
Lustre powders and large selection of
paints

Creative Beadcraft,
20 Beak Street,
London W1F 9RE
020 7629 9964
www.creativebeadcraft.co.uk
Huge selection of beads and
jewellery wire

John Lewis,
Oxford Street,
London W1A 1EX
020 7629 7711
www.johnlewis.com
Great for haberdashery, beads,
glue and fabric

Liberty,
Great Marlborough Street,
London W1B 5AH
020 7743 1234
www.liberty.co.uk
Lovely selection of buttons and fabrics

London Bead Shop,
24 Earlham Street,
London WC2H 9LN
020 7379 9214
www.londonbeadshop.co.uk
Wide selection of beads and accessories

Paperchase,
213-215 Tottenham Court Road,
London W1T 7PS
0161-839 1500 for mail order
www.paperchase.co.uk
Glues, papers, paints and art materials

Alec Tiranti,
27 Warren Street,
London W1T 5NB
0845 123 2100
www.tiranti.co.uk
Metallic foils in silver, gold and copper

VV Rouleaux,
102 Marylebone Lane,
London W1V 2QD,
020 7224 5179
www.vvrouleaux.com
Fabulous selection of ribbons

index

For Laurie Dahl. Here's to lots more lovely Christmases together.

I would like to thank the following people for their help with this book:
Debbie Patterson for the beautiful photography and for getting into the Christmas
spirit so well and Michael Hill for creating such lovely illustrations.

Roger Hammond for the great design and to Marion Paull for being an all round
lovely editor. Sally Powell at CICO for all the help and support given and to Cindy
Richards for commissioning me to do this book in the first place and encouraging
my glittery side to come out.

And finally to Laurie, Gracie and Betty for all the encouragement, support and love
given during our extended 'Christmas'. Thank you, my loves.